A Weekend Off

by Carmel Reilly

illustrated by James Rey Sanchez

T0362664

OXFORD
UNIVERSITY PRESS
AUSTRALIA & NEW ZEALAND

Chapter 1
A busy week

"I'm so glad it's Friday," said Emma, flopping onto the couch after dinner.

"Goodness me, yes," said Mum, "What a busy week!"

"It's always so busy," said Dad, slumping beside them. "I feel like I never stop."

"Me too!" cried Ted, jumping on Dad's knee.

"I feel so tired," said Mum. "All I seem to do is race between work, Grandma, the animals, the garden and loads of chores."

"And I am always rushing around. I have so many after-school lessons, like gym, drama, dance and tuba," said Emma.

"Me too," said Ted.

One judo session a week is plenty for me!

"We should try and have a super-relaxing time this weekend," said Emma.

"Good plan," said Dad. "What relaxing things would you like to do?"

"I'd love to hang out with my friends and watch a funny movie at home," said Emma.

"Cooking something special would be fun," said Mum.

"I want to go shopping," said Ted. "I've nearly run out of Mini Bricks."

Dad nodded. "It's going to be warm tomorrow. Why don't we start with a long walk. Then we can pick up your bricks later on."

— Chapter 2 —
Time to start relaxing

On Saturday morning, Emma was woken up by a loud noise.
It was Dad just outside her bedroom.

"Morning!" he cried. "Time to start our relaxing weekend.
It's a lovely sunny day for a walk," he said.

Emma sat up and rubbed her eyes.

After a quick bowl of oats, they drove to a nearby park.

"Isn't this wonderful?" said Dad, striding off.

"I'm a bit cold," said Emma.

"We'll warm up if we move faster," replied Dad, cheerfully.

— Chapter 3 —
Pancakes

"I'm hungry," said Ted, when the walk was over.

"Let's go home and I'll make pancakes," said Mum. "I love making pancakes!"

"Yay!" said Ted.

They started to walk to the car, when Mum suddenly stopped.

"We need eggs," she said.

They drove to the supermarket. "I need to buy some more things for dinner tonight, too," said Mum. "Who wants to give me a hand?"

"Can we get some fruit?" asked Emma, as the four of them went inside.

"And some treats?" added Ted, bounding towards the biscuit aisle.

Back at home, Dad and the children unpacked the shopping. Mum quickly cooked a batch of pancakes and cut up passionfruit to put on top.

"Oh yummy!" said Emma. "I love passionfruit."

"Me too," said Ted.

Really, I love bananas the best.

"The morning has gone quickly," said Dad as they finished eating. "Look at the time."

Emma stared up at the clock. "Oh no!" she squealed. "Maya's party is this afternoon and I don't have a present."

"We had better go and get one, then," said Dad.

"And don't forget I need to get bricks!" said Ted.

— Chapter 4 —
A shopping trip

The family drove to the shopping centre. Dad took Emma to a gift shop to get a present for her friend. It didn't take long for Emma to find a lovely scarf with a giraffe pattern around the edge.

"Maya will love this," she said. "She loves giraffes."

In the meantime, Mum took Ted to a toy shop. Ted found the bricks he wanted.

He also saw a chess set that he liked. "You'll need to save up for that," said Mum.

Then she glanced down at Ted's feet. "What you do need right now is a new pair of shoes."

Mum and Ted met Dad and Emma outside the toy shop.

"We need to get new shoes for Ted," said Mum.

"While you do that, I'll drop Emma at Maya's party," said Dad. "Then I'll come back and pick you up."

"See you soon," said Mum.

Mum and Ted went into the first sports shop they found. Ted felt one of the shoes on display. "These feel really hard," he said.

"They will feel better when you wear them a few times," said Mum. He picked up another shoe. "This one doesn't smell very nice."

Mum and Ted walked to another sports shop, but it was very busy. There was a long queue outside.

Mum raised her eyebrows. "I don't think we'll be going there," she said.

At the far end of the centre they found a children's shoe shop. Ted was excited about lots of the things he saw on display.

He tried on five pairs before he decided on some with a blue sole.

Mum phoned Dad. "Mission completed. You can come and pick us up now!"

Chapter 5
Dinner time

Dad fetched Mum and Ted and dropped them at home. Then he went off to pick up Emma. Mum started preparing dinner, while Ted ran in circles around the garden.

"I love these shoes!" he shouted.

Soon, Dad returned with Emma. When she saw Ted outside, she ran out to play with him. Moments later, they were on the trampoline, jumping and giggling loudly.

Dad took over the cooking from Mum while she fed the cat and the dog, and phoned Grandma. Ted and Emma came inside and set the table.

Then they helped Dad carry the dinner dishes out from the kitchen.

After dinner, Ted and Emma helped Mum and Dad clean up. Dad put the kettle on to make a pot of tea.

"Who would like an ice cream?" called Mum.

"You know I love ice cream better than any other food," said Emma.

"Me too," said Ted, who really did love ice cream the best, too.

— Chapter 6 —
Back to the couch

Ted and Emma leapt onto the couch. Dad walked in carrying bowls of ice cream.

"Your turn to pick a movie, Emma," he said.

"I want to watch something funny tonight," said Emma, grabbing the remote control.

"Me too!" said Ted.

I always love watching funny movies!

Everyone squeezed in together on the couch.

"Goodness, what a day," said Mum, kicking off her shoes.

"I thought we could have a really relaxing day!" said Dad, but it turned out to be just as busy as every other day!"

"It has been fun," said Mum. "And I do feel quite relaxed now ..."

"I'm so relaxed I could almost fall asleep," said Emma, yawning.

"Me too," said Ted, whose eyes had already closed.